I'M GOOD AT
HISTORY
WHAT JOB CAN I GET?

Kelly Davis

Published in paperback in 2014 by Wayland
Copyright Wayland 2014

Wayland
Hachette Children's Books
338 Euston Road
London NW1 3BH

Wayland Australia
Level 17/207 Kent Street,
Sydney, NSW 2000

Commissioning editor: Victoria Brooker
Project editor: Kelly Davis
Designer: Tim Mayer
Picture research: Kelly Davis
Proofreader: Alice Harman

Produced for Wayland by
White-Thomson Publishing Ltd
www.wtpub.co.uk
+44 (0)843 2087 460

British Library Cataloguing in Publication Data

Davis, Kelly, 1959-
I'm good at history - what job can I get?.
1. History–Vocational guidance–Juvenile
literature.
I. Title
902.3-dc23

ISBN-13: 9780750281829

Printed in China

10 9 8 7 6 5 4 3 2 1

Wayland is a division of Hachette Children's Books, an Hachette UK company
www.hachette.co.uk

Picture credits
1, Shutterstock/corepics; 3, Shutterstock/
Marques; 4, Dreamstime/jblackstock;
5, Shutterstock/Mikhail Shiyanov; 6/7,
Shutterstock/Stephen Inglis; 7, Shutterstock/
Denton Rumsey; 8, Shutterstock/shock; 9,
Shutterstock/spaxiax; 10, Wikipedia; 11,
Shutterstock/pio3; 12, Shutterstock/corepics;
13, Shutterstock/Zurijeta; 14, Wikipedia; 15,
Shutterstock/Marques; 16, Shutterstock/
leedsn; 17, Shutterstock/AISPIX by Image
Source; 18, Dreamstime/Carloscastilla; 19,
Shutterstock/1000Words; 20, Shutterstock/
Stephen Coburn; 21, Shutterstock/Nata-Lia; 22
Shutterstock/AVAVA; 23, Shutterstock/Monkey
Business Images; 24, Shutterstock/mangostock;
25, Shutterstock/Monkey Business Images;
26, Shutterstock/pryzmat; 27, Dreamstime/
Robeo; 28, Shutterstock/Natalia Mikhaylova; 29,
Shutterstock/Czesznak Zsolt; cover (top left),
Shutterstock/Mikhail Shiyanov; cover (top right),
Wikipedia; cover (bottom), Wikipedia.

Disclaimer
The website addresses (URLs) included in this
book were valid at the time of going to press.
However, because of the nature of the Internet,
it is possible that some addresses may have
changed, or sites may have changed or closed
down since publication. While the author and
Publisher regret any inconvenience this may
cause the readers, no responsibility for any such
changes can be accepted by either the author or
Publisher.

CONTENTS

The world of history

History is the story of what happened in the past. Above all, it involves relationships – between rulers and their people, between countries and cultures, and between past and present. Winston Churchill (prime minister of Britain during the Second World War) said 'Those that fail to learn from history, are doomed to repeat it', and this is perhaps one of the most important reasons for studying this subject.

We are surrounded by history in our towns and cities. Here, a carved monster on the twelfth-century Notre Dame Cathedral looks down on modern Paris.

History graduates have a wide range of skills and are therefore highly valued by employers in many different areas, including heritage, research, politics, law, government, the media and education. Some universities offer degrees that combine history with subjects such as modern languages, economics and politics, and these courses can provide good preparation for particular careers.

History in the workplace

Some jobs, such as heritage manager or museum conservator, require specific historical knowledge. Other jobs make indirect use of some of the skills needed to study history. For example, lawyers need to be able to construct a clear, persuasive argument using relevant evidence, and trade union researchers have to use research skills to find the information they need for particular media campaigns.

Special skills

To do a history or combined history degree, you should aim to get a high score in the International Baccalaureate or three good A-levels. For most universities, these will need to include an A or A* in history. If you are good at history, you will be able to apply reason and logic, ask questions and negotiate, discuss and debate issues (taking many different factors into account), research, collect and analyse data, construct arguments and express them clearly, and communicate well – both in speech and writing.

↑ Studying history gives us an insight into what life was like in another time and place – such as ancient Rome, where even a powerful emperor like Julius Caesar could fall victim to a murder plot.

PROFESSIONAL VIEWPOINT

'Without history we are infants. Ask what binds the British Isles more closely to America than to Europe and only history gives a reply. Of all intellectual pursuits, history is the most supremely useful. That is why people crave it and need ever more of it.'
Simon Jenkins, journalist, author and Chairman of the National Trust

Heritage manager

Places and objects that were built or made by previous generations are part of our heritage. Whether it is a historic house, an ancient monument, or the traditions or culture of a particular region, our heritage needs to be managed and protected. Heritage managers have to generate income from historic sites – for example, through entrance fees, donations, selling souvenirs and hiring out sites for filming. At the same time, they have to preserve the authentic character of the site.

Job description

Heritage managers:

- generate income from heritage sites
- apply for grants and sponsorship
- arrange maintenance and conservation of sites
- recruit and monitor staff and volunteers
- promote heritage sites using local and national media
- ensure that health and safety standards are met
- design and analyse visitor feedback surveys
- develop partnerships with local authorities, tourist boards, funding bodies and other heritage organisations.

↓ Stonehenge on Salisbury Plain, Wiltshire, is a world-famous ancient site. Heritage managers are planning to improve visitors' experience by building an information centre nearby.

In the UK, English Heritage looks after more than 400 historic sites, and the National Trust cares for over 300 buildings and gardens in England, Wales and Northern Ireland. There are other heritage organisations looking after hundreds of sites in Scotland. Heritage managers may also work for local authorities, tourist boards and private consultancies.

What skills do I need?

You will need a degree, preferably in history or history of art, archaeology, heritage or museum studies, countryside or estate management, or marketing. You should also have a real enthusiasm for heritage and be a skilful and effective communicator and negotiator. Most importantly, you should be able to offer relevant experience. The best way to get this is by volunteering or by taking a holiday job as a visitor reception assistant.

PROFESSIONAL VIEWPOINT
'I look after a famous National Trust property. Our guides have to wear Victorian costume and I keep an eye on them to make sure that every detail is correct. I also brief them thoroughly so that they can answer all the visitors' questions.'
Charlotte, heritage manager

↑ Heritage managers may get requests from members of historical re-enactment groups, like these American Civil War history enthusiasts, to use a particular site.

Information officer

If you are keen on history, you will be used to searching through information and selecting the relevant facts when carrying out research for your essays. These research skills can be extremely useful because information plays a central part in most activities in today's society. Information officers are also known as information managers or information scientists. Much of their work involves electronic databases and the Internet. They find and manage the information needed by an organisation or client to fulfil particular aims.

↑ Laptop computers are vital tools for information officers.

The British National Archives (see page 31) has millions of documents and images in its collection, covering 1,000 years of history, and offers a number of history-related information management job opportunities. However, there are many other companies and organisations that also employ information officers. These include banks, insurance firms, law firms, charities, political parties, healthcare organisations, manufacturers and government departments.

PROFESSIONAL VIEWPOINT
'I work at the National Archives, where we "create history" by recording events as they happen. For example, I was helping to record and catalogue the London 2012 Olympics and Paralympics while the Games were actually happening. We've created an Olympic Record website, where the public can contribute information to help us build a complete picture for future generations.'
Mahmud, information officer

What skills do I need?

You can enter this field with a degree in any subject, but employers will favour graduates in librarianship or information management. If you would like to be an information officer for a charity or political organisation, a history degree will be helpful but you will also need a postgraduate qualification accredited by the Chartered Institute of Library and Information Professionals (see page 31). Strong computing and IT skills are vital. You should also be good at communicating with colleagues and other professionals, carrying out research, working carefully and accurately, and keeping up to date with the latest IT developments.

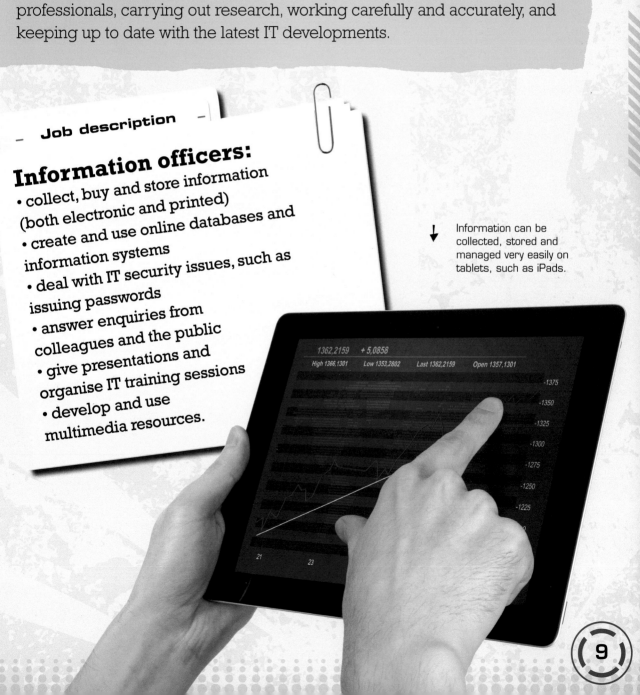

Job description

Information officers:

- collect, buy and store information (both electronic and printed)
- create and use online databases and information systems
- deal with IT security issues, such as issuing passwords
- answer enquiries from colleagues and the public
- give presentations and organise IT training sessions
- develop and use multimedia resources.

↓ Information can be collected, stored and managed very easily on tablets, such as iPads.

1362,2159   + 5,0858
High 1366,1301   Low 1353,2802   Last 1362,2159   Open 1357,1301

Museum conservator

Imagine spending your working week surrounded by beautiful paintings and sculptures that were created hundreds of years ago. These rare and valuable objects can be damaged by wear and tear, insects, temperature and humidity. As a conservator, you would be responsible for restoring and preserving them so that the public can enjoy seeing them – both now and in the future.

↑ Textile conservation often requires a high level of technical skill.

PROFESSIONAL VIEWPOINT

'I work on seventeenth-century paintings at the Victoria and Albert Museum. I have to clean them extremely carefully, using cotton swabs. It's slow, painstaking work but nothing can beat the thrill of seeing the original colours emerge from under the old brown varnish.'

Paul, painting conservator

Conservators use a combination of scientific and artistic techniques. Some conservators work with a wide range of objects. Others become expert in a particular field, such as ceramics, painting, textiles or furniture. A number of conservators are employed by museums and galleries. Others are self-employed and work for museums on a freelance (self-employed) basis, as well as for private collectors, antique dealers, and auction houses such as Christie's and Sotheby's.

Conservators:

- examine objects to assess damage
- photograph objects and record any restoration previously carried out
- check storage and display conditions to ensure that objects are not damaged any further
- work out a restoration budget
- communicate with other conservators
- find the best ways of cleaning and repairing objects, using special tools and traditional materials
- research new conservation methods.

The Victoria and Albert Museum, which houses the world's largest decorative arts and design collection, employs several museum conservators.

What skills do I need?

Ideally, you will have a degree in art conservation or art history, but employers may also favour archaeology, museum studies, chemistry and biology graduates. Most museums and galleries will also expect some museum experience (whether paid or voluntary) and a relevant postgraduate qualification. You can find information about postgraduate courses on the Institute of Conservation website (see page 31). A good conservator will be very patient and careful, with a genuine interest in history and art. The specific practical skills required will depend on the area you specialise in.

Academic librarian

If you like history, you probably love reading and finding things out using research techniques. As an academic librarian, you can make use of all these skills and enjoy working in the interesting, stimulating atmosphere of a university, further education college or research institute.

Academic librarians are often responsible for a particular subject, and they offer support to teaching staff from that department – helping them draw up reading lists for their students and sometimes even assisting with course development. They also help researchers and students locate the materials they need. The job involves managing electronic resources (including databases and web pages) as well as printed books and journals.

↑ A librarian with a cheerful, helpful manner can encourage staff and students to make use of the library.

What skills do I need?

A-levels in subjects like history, English, maths and computer studies will enable you to get into university to study librarianship, information science or computing. To secure a professional academic librarian's post, you will then need to do a postgraduate qualification approved by the Chartered Institute of Library and Information Professionals (see page 31). Having done some voluntary work in your local public library will make you a stronger candidate. You will need to be good at communicating and dealing with a wide range of people and have excellent IT skills. You will also have to be flexible and able to work under pressure in a busy academic environment.

↑ If reading is one of your favourite occupations, academic librarianship may well be the right career for you.

Job description

Academic librarians:
- deal with enquiries from students and staff
- manage the library budget
- catalogue and update information, using computer software
- communicate with academic departments
- order new resources for the library
- help researchers carry out literature searches
- recruit and manage library staff
- offer information skills training sessions.

Archaeologist

Imagine discovering an ancient altar buried deep underground, or unearthing a piece of pottery that hasn't been touched by another person for several centuries! If you like the idea of finding evidence to show how people lived in the past, archaeology may well be the job for you.

PROFESSIONAL VIEWPOINT

'I particularly enjoy seeing different parts of the country and getting to know the local people. I was at a site last month when one of the volunteers suddenly found some bone fragments. He was jumping up and down with excitement! We think the fragments are from a sixth-century burial and we're sending them off to the laboratory to get the date confirmed.'

Greg, archaeologist

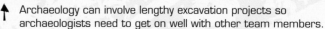
Archaeology can involve lengthy excavation projects so archaeologists need to get on well with other team members.

What skills do I need?

You are more likely to get a job as an archaeologist if you are a graduate – preferably in archaeology, ancient history, conservation or heritage management. For some types of archaeology, a science or computer studies degree may also be very useful. If you want to teach at a university or specialise in a particular type of archaeology, you will also need a postgraduate qualification. Being physically fit and having a driving licence will ensure that you can work outdoors and travel. It will also help if you are a patient, practical, enthusiastic person, with an enquiring mind and good IT skills.

Archaeologists don't just dig holes in the ground. They also work in universities and museums and for organisations such as English Heritage, the National Trust and the Environment Agency. There is a lot of competition for jobs in archaeology so it's important to show your commitment early on by doing voluntary archaeological work – for example, by helping at a museum or joining an excavation (or 'dig').

↑ Archaeologists will sometimes be rewarded with an amazing discovery – like this jar of ancient Greek coins, found in the ruins of Ampurias, in Spain.

Job description

Archaeologists:
- arrange for proposed sites to be examined using geophysical surveys and aerial photography
- excavate sites, with other team members
- make notes and take photographs of sites
- examine and interpret archaeological artefacts (or 'finds') to date them and work out how they were used
- clean and preserve artefacts
- arrange for important sites and monuments to be protected
- produce reports, articles and presentations on archaeological discoveries
- help to display artefacts
- teach archaeology students.

Politician's assistant

If you like history, you may well take a keen interest in politics. As a politician's assistant, you will be able to see what life is like behind the newspaper headlines, at the heart of government. A politician's assistant provides secretarial, promotional and research support to elected politicians, to enable them to represent their constituents effectively. It's an interesting, exciting job for people who are good at multi-tasking and coping with pressure.

PROFESSIONAL VIEWPOINT

'I did a combined history and politics degree, and I made sure I did a lot of networking at university. That definitely paid off because contacts are so important in this field. Since I started working at Westminster, I've found that I already know a number of other political researchers and journalists.'

Silvana, politician's assistant

You could end up working for a Member of Parliament (MP) in London or a Member of the European Parliament (MEP) in Strasbourg. There are also opportunities to assist politicians in Scotland, Wales and Northern Ireland. This is a competitive field so you will need to show your enthusiasm by getting involved in student politics while you are at university and then volunteering or doing an internship for a political party or non-governmental organisation (NGO).

A politician's assistant needs constant Internet access so a laptop computer is essential.

Politicians expect their assistants to brief them before radio and television interviews and discussions.

Job description

Politician's assistants:

- deal with enquiries from the public, other politicians and pressure groups
- make travel arrangements, fill in the politician's diary and take minutes at meetings
- write leaflets and newsletters
- arrange media interviews
- help to write speeches and reports
- accompany the politician to public events
- help with election campaigns.

What skills do I need?

You will need a degree, preferably in history, politics, government, economics, international relations, law or social policy. A postgraduate qualification is not vital but could strengthen your application for certain posts. Good IT skills are essential and an ability to speak French or German will be helpful if you want to work for an MEP. A politician's assistant needs many personal qualities, including confidence, professionalism, tact, discretion, reliability and a genuine interest in politics. You should also be good at communicating and working with other people.

Trade union researcher

Are you particularly interested in social history, which tells the story of ordinary working people? If so, you will know that trade unions are organisations formed by workers in a particular trade to negotiate fair wages and working conditions. If you have a strong belief in social justice, a career as a trade union researcher may be the perfect choice.

PROFESSIONAL VIEWPOINT

'I work with a small team of researchers at the GMB London office and I've learned that you need to have the facts at your fingertips to put together a convincing presentation. Recently, we've been helping to organise campaigns against racism and bullying in the workplace. I'm proud of the work I do – I feel we're helping to change things for the better.'

Simon, trade union researcher

Job description

Trade union researchers:

• research social, economic, industrial and political issues that affect union members
• collect data that can be used in negotiations and media campaigns
• assess the impact of new employment laws
• produce reports on which union officials base new policies
• prepare speeches and presentations
• write trade union recruitment leaflets
• help to organise trade union conferences and training sessions.

Trade union researchers need to be able to analyse statistics and produce graphs.

↑ Some trade unions have a lot of support. An estimated 250,000 people took part in this TUC-organised rally against government cuts in 2011.

The larger unions employ several researchers to provide information on which they base their activities and campaigns. Although trade union membership has declined since the late 1970s, trade unions are still some of the biggest organisations in Britain. For example, UNISON represents 1.3 million people who work in education and public services, and there are 58 British trade unions (with a total of 6.5 million members) that belong to the Trades Union Congress (TUC).

What skills do I need?

A degree is vital to secure a researcher's position, and graduates in history, politics, sociology, law or economics will have an advantage. A postgraduate qualification will be helpful, especially if it requires you to study research methods and statistics. You should have a strong commitment to the ideals of the trade union movement and a keen interest in politics. You should also have an up-to-date knowledge of the issues affecting members of your particular trade union. Writing, presenting, IT and research skills are also vital. You can strengthen your application by gaining experience with your student union at university.

Lawyer

Historians frequently hold opposing views on historical questions. If you enjoy arguments and debates, you may want to become a lawyer. Having a logical, analytical mind, enjoying research and being good at public speaking are all qualities that could also mean you are very suited to a legal career.

You have to spend several years studying and training to become a lawyer but, once you are qualified, it is a very respected, well-paid profession. →

What skills do I need?

You will need good grades to study law at university, and history would be a sensible choice for one of your A-levels. After graduating, you will have to take a one-year Legal Practice Course (LPC), followed by a Professional Skills Course (PSC). Alternatively, you could take a degree in a subject other than law, do a one-year conversion course and then follow the same training as a law graduate (the LPC and the PSC). Some would-be solicitors are recruited by law firms before they start their third year at university. The law firm then pays for their postgraduate training. Becoming a solicitor requires confidence, commitment, professionalism and attention to detail, as well as excellent writing and speaking skills and a knowledge of IT.

Solicitors have to point out any possible problems before their clients agree to the terms of a contract.

Different types of lawyer

Solicitors advise individuals on buying property, making a will, getting divorced and other matters. They also advise companies on commercial disputes. Barristers are usually hired by solicitors to plead (argue) a case in court, on behalf of an individual or organisation. Around 80 per cent of barristers are self-employed and work in chambers (lawyers' offices). Others work for the Crown Prosecution Service (CPS). Most barristers specialise in a particular type of law, such as commercial (business), chancery (property), common (personal injury and family law) or criminal (burglary and other crimes).

PROFESSIONAL VIEWPOINT

'I'm with a small, high-street firm at present – and I prefer it to the commercial law firm where I did my previous placement. I enjoy being part of the community and building up a personal relationship with my clients. It's particularly important to gain their trust when you're dealing with sensitive issues like divorce.'

Jameela, solicitor

Job description

Solicitors:
- advise clients on legal issues
- write letters and contracts
- research case law and documents
- instruct barristers
- occasionally represent clients in court
- work out claims for damages and compensation.

History teacher

If you love history, you probably like the idea of bringing it to life for others. Perhaps you want to help children develop an understanding of the Second World War? Or maybe you like the idea of teaching them how British society has changed over the past few centuries?

Primary schools usually concentrate on the core skills of numeracy and literacy, with only occasional coverage of history topics. As a specialist history teacher, you are therefore more likely to work in a secondary school, teaching children aged 11 to 18. You could also work in a sixth form college or further education college.

↑ History teachers need to emphasise essay-writing skills, such as presenting an argument, supporting it with evidence and drawing a conclusion.

Job description

History teachers:
- write lively, interesting lesson plans
- teach lessons, using a variety of resources
- keep up to date with curriculum developments
- monitor pupils' progress and mark their work
- organise school trips to historic sites
- communicate with teaching colleagues and parents
- manage pupils' behaviour.

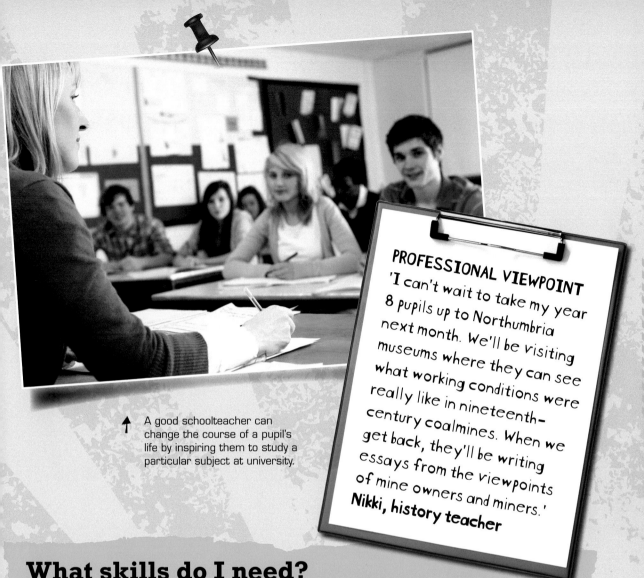

A good schoolteacher can change the course of a pupil's life by inspiring them to study a particular subject at university.

PROFESSIONAL VIEWPOINT
'I can't wait to take my year 8 pupils up to Northumbria next month. We'll be visiting museums where they can see what working conditions were really like in nineteenth-century coalmines. When we get back, they'll be writing essays from the viewpoints of mine owners and miners.'
Nikki, history teacher

What skills do I need?

There are several ways of becoming a history teacher. You can take a history degree and then do initial teacher training (ITT) or a Postgraduate Certificate of Education (PGCE) for a year. Alternatively, you can study for your degree and complete your ITT at the same time. Taking the Bachelor of Arts (BA) with qualified teacher status (QTS) will enable you to specialise in history. If you would rather teach in primary schools, you could do the general Bachelor of Education (BEd) honours degree. Most importantly, you should have a real enthusiasm for history. Like all teachers, you also need to have strong leadership skills and be well organised and good at communicating. Being patient and self-confident will help you cope with challenging pupils. You can gain experience of working with children by doing private tutoring or helping at a play scheme, youth club or summer camp.

Charity fundraiser

If you have an urge to work for good causes as well as an interest in history, you may be able to combine the two by becoming a charity fundraiser. Some charitable organisations, such as the National Trust (see page 31), are keen to recruit people who have studied history at university. Other charities that are active in the developing world, such as Oxfam or UNICEF, may value workers with a particular knowledge of African or Asian history.

PROFESSIONAL VIEWPOINT

'After I left university, I spent a few months doing voluntary work in the Gambia. When that ended, I came back to the UK but I still wanted to do something to help people in the developing world. My experience as a volunteer helped me get my present job as a community fundraiser for Oxfam, which I absolutely love.'

Joanne, charity fundraiser

→ Charity fundraisers need to be good at thinking of ideas to raise money for charity. Clothes can be sold or they can be donated directly to those who need them.

DONATIONS

Charity fundraisers:

- make people aware of the charity through publicity
- inspire supporters to raise money
- organise fundraising events, sponsored activities and collections of donated items
- develop the charity's website and online fundraising
- recruit volunteers to help the charity
- maintain databases of donors' contact details
- send out mail-shots to encourage donations
- develop corporate sponsorship.

↑ Charity fundraisers still make use of traditional methods, such as collecting tins in shops and businesses.

Different types of charity fundraiser

Community fundraisers raise money from the general public through collections and fundraising events and activities, while corporate fundraisers encourage companies to make charitable donations through corporate sponsorship and employee donations. Trust fundraisers apply for funds from trusts and grant-giving organsations, and major donor fundraisers develop relationships with individual supporters who are able to make very large donations. Finally, legacy fundraisers encourage supporters to leave charitable legacies in their wills.

What skills do I need?

A degree in history may be helpful, as will postgraduate qualifications in marketing, media, international development, business studies and events management. It is vital to have some previous voluntary experience with a charity, and some of the bigger charitable organisations offer internships that can lead to permanent jobs. Enthusiasm, sensitivity and a strong belief in the charitable cause are all important qualities for fundraisers. You also need to be a natural communicator, who can build good relationships with donors and volunteers.

Historic buildings inspector

Do you love visiting old buildings, where you can see how people used to live hundreds of years ago? If you are interested in architecture as well as history, you may enjoy helping to conserve some of the many sites of special historic, artistic or architectural interest that exist throughout England, Scotland, Wales and Northern Ireland. These can range from small Victorian workers' cottages to huge stately homes, and from a single building to a whole street that needs regeneration.

↑ Historic buildings inspectors need to find people with the skills required to carry out complex restoration work.

PROFESSIONAL VIEWPOINT

'I love seeing the transformation from a dusty, collapsing ruin to a beautiful building that has been restored and will be there for future generations to enjoy. It sometimes takes years to see that result but it makes all the hard work worthwhile.'

Sally, historic buildings inspector

Around 50 per cent of historic buildings inspectors (also known as conservation officers) work for private construction firms and consultancies. The rest work for central government, local authorities and organisations such as English Heritage and the National Trust (see page 31).

Historic buildings inspectors:

- assess and recommend conservation and regeneration projects
- advise on planning applications to ensure that historic buildings are protected
- work with local authorities and heritage and conservation organisations
- ensure that health and safety regulations are followed on site
- communicate with local people and find out what they think
- manage long-term conservation projects
- find craftspeople who can use traditional tools and materials
- apply for conservation grants.

Inspectors visit the site to note down the work required. They may also need to visit during the project and after it is complete.

What skills do I need?

You will need a degree, ideally in building conservation, planning, civil or structural engineering, or architecture. However, a number of buildings inspectors study history, architectural history, art history or archaeology at university, followed by a relevant postgraduate qualification approved by the Institute of Historic Building Conservation (see page 31). Historic buildings inspectors need to have a real interest in historic buildings and construction techniques, and a good knowledge of the law relating to building and conservation. A driving licence and excellent communication, numeracy, IT and project management skills will also be very useful.

Historical writer

Do you enjoy reading historical novels that plunge you into life at court in Elizabethan times or make you feel that you are marching to battle with a Roman legion? History is recorded through writing, and historians can use their expert knowledge to produce biographies, historical non-fiction and historical novels. They may sometimes advise on television and film scripts for historical dramas. Some professional historians, such as Mary Beard and Simon Schama, have become well-known television and radio presenters as well as authors.

PROFESSIONAL VIEWPOINT

'I would advise any would-be writer to buy a copy of the *Writers' and Artists' Yearbook*, which gives details of all the publishers and agents in the UK and gives good advice on how to submit a manuscript. I found my publisher that way. They signed me up to write a series of historical biographies and I've been working on those for the last couple of years.'
Jeremy, author

↓ World-famous author Hilary Mantel won the 2009 Man Booker Prize for her historical novel *Wolf Hall*, based on the life of Henry VIII's right-hand man Thomas Cromwell.

The Man Booker Prize 2009

What skills do I need?

Many historical writers are graduates in English literature, history, creative writing, journalism or media studies. If you wish to write for television, film or radio, you will need to do a specialist scriptwriting or screenwriting course. To succeed as a historical writer, talent, imagination, a good writing style, self-discipline and determination are sometimes more important than academic qualifications. However, you will definitely need strong research and IT skills.

Historical writers often have to visit libraries to research original sources such as hand-written letters and diaries.

Thorough research is vital for all historical writing, as readers want to know the details of life in the past – what people ate, how they travelled, what they wore, how they spoke, and so on. Most historical writers are self-employed and often combine their writing with teaching and other types of employment. Some may get contracts with book publishers and some work freelance, producing text for websites and magazine or newspaper articles.

Job description

Historical writers:

- research the subject of their books or articles
- use research to check facts
- develop their writing skills so that their characters and plots are convincing
- manage their time and meet deadlines
- deal with publishers, editors and agents
- negotiate fees and contracts
- make public appearances to promote their writing.

Glossary

aerial photography photographs taken from an aircraft or spacecraft

analyse study or examine in detail

artefact object made by human beings in the past

auction house place where people gather to buy goods, which are sold to the person who offers the most money

authentic true or genuine

biography story of a person's life, written by someone else

ceramics pots, tiles and other objects made of baked clay

constituent voter in an area (constituency), represented by a Member of Parliament (MP)

culture attitudes, customs and behaviour of a particular group of people

data factual information

elect choose a politician to become a Member of Parliament by voting for them

English Heritage organisation set up to protect and promote England's historic environment

excavation hole dug by archaeologists

freelance self-employed and working for several different clients or organisations

geophysical survey map of underground archaeological features, made using instruments that can detect differences between soil and other substances such as metal and wood

humidity dampness; water vapour in the air

internship practical work experience for people who want to go into a particular profession

legacy something passed on or left behind by someone or something

marketing type of business concerned with publicity, promotion and advertising

minutes official written record of what is said in a meeting

multimedia resources digital or computerised resources that include words, images and sound

multi-tasking carrying out several tasks at the same time

National Trust organisation set up to preserve historic buildings and areas of great beauty in England, Wales and Northern Ireland

networking establishing mutually beneficial friendships with people who may be helpful to you in your profession

non-governmental organisation (NGO) non-profit-making organisation with social or political aims, such as a charity, community group or campaigning organisation

pressure group group of people that tries to influence public opinion and government policy

regeneration redevelopment, renewal or rebuilding of part of a town or city

textiles fabrics, such as silk or cotton, made by weaving threads

Further information

There are many specific courses and jobs using history skills, so where do you go to find out more? It is really useful to meet up with careers advisers at school or college and to attend careers fairs to see the range of opportunities. Remember that public libraries and newspapers are other important sources of information. The earlier you check out your options, the better prepared you will be to put your history skills to good use as you earn a living in future.

Books

Law Uncovered (Careers Uncovered)
Margaret McAlpine, Trotman & Co Ltd, 2009

Teaching Uncovered (Careers Uncovered)
Karen Holmes, Trotman & Co Ltd, 2010

The A-Z of Careers and Jobs
Susan Hodgson, Kogan Page, 2012

Top Careers for History Graduates
Checkmark Books, Facts on File, 2004

What Next After School?: All You Need to Know About Work, Travel and Study,
Elizabeth Holmes, Kogan Page, 2012

Websites

www.prospects.ac.uk/options_history_job_options.htm
A very useful guide to history-related careers, with a comprehensive list of resources and contacts.

www.history.org.uk/resources/public_resource_2914_76.html
The Historical Association website has some helpful careers advice.

www.cilip.org.uk/jobs-careers/careers-gateway/pages/default.aspx
The Chartered Institute of Library and Information Professionals website.

www.education.gov.uk/get-into-teaching
The Department for Education Teaching Agency website offers guidance on different routes into teaching.

www.english-heritage.org.uk/caring/get-involved/volunteering
The English Heritage website gives advice on volunteering.

www.icon.org.uk
The website for the Institute of Conservation, the lead voice for the conservation of cultural heritage in the UK. Click on 'Career planning'.

www.ihbc.org.uk
The Institute of Historic Buildings Conservation website.

www.lawsociety.org.uk/home.law
The Law Society website. Click on 'Careers in law'.

www.nationalarchives.gov.uk
National Archives website. See information on careers and volunteering.

www.nationaltrustjobs.org.uk/about_us
The National Trust website. Click on 'Career development'.

Index